Daughter, Daedalus

Winner of the 2016 T. S. Eliot Prize

The T. S. Eliot Prize for Poetry is an annual award sponsored by Truman State University Press for the best unpublished book-length collection of poetry in English, in honor of native Missourian T. S. Eliot's considerable intellectual and artistic legacy.

Judge: Jennifer Clement.

Jennifer Clement is the author of four poetry collections: *The Next Stranger* (with an introduction by W. S. Merwin), *Newton's Sailor*, *Lady of the Broom*, and *Jennifer Clement: New and Selected Poems*. She is also the author of three novels—*Prayers for the Stolen*, *A True Story Based on Lies*, and *The Poison That Fascinates*—and the acclaimed memoir *Widow Basquiat*. Her prize-winning story "A Salamander-Child" is published as an art book with work by the Mexican painter Gustavo Monroy. Clement's books have been translated into twenty-four languages.

Daughter, Daedalus

Alison D. Moncrief Bromage

New Odyssey Series
Truman State University Press
Kirksville, Missouri

Cover art: F. Bereude, *Landes—Echassier et Bergere*, postcard, ca. early 1900s
(author's collection).
Cover design: Lisa Ahrens

Library of Congress Cataloging-in-Publication Data

Names: Moncrief Bromage, Alison D., author.
Title: Daughter, Daedalus / by Alison D. Moncrief Bromage.
Description: Kirksville, Missouri : Truman State University Press, 2016. |
  Series: New Odyssey series | Description based on print version record and
  CIP data provided by publisher; resource not viewed.
Identifiers: LCCN 2016026797 (print) | LCCN 2016026476 (ebook) | ISBN
  9781612481845 () | ISBN 9781612481838 (pbk. : alk. paper)
Classification: LCC PS3613.O52356 (print) | LCC PS3613.O52356 A6 2016
  (ebook)
  | DDC 811/.6--dc23
LC record available at https://lccn.loc.gov/2016026797

For my parents, Eileen and Bill Moncrief

Contents

Limbo

Daughter, The Prologue

Acknowledgments

Grateful acknowledgment to the editors of the following publications who printed the following poems, sometimes in different iterations:

The Paris Review: "Prologue"

Denver Quarterly: "Twin A" (published as "Fever Shed")

Barrow Street: "We Come and Go in Ships" and "The Dancing Place"

The Bennington Review: "About Silence"

Copper Nickel: "Gravity"

After Happy Hour Review: "Father of Invention"

fields: "Firsts Born"

2 River Review: "Daughter, you will sleep on a sheepskin"; "The butchers will slaughter"; "Of the family line"; "Where we come from"; and "At the edge of the yard, the milkweed pods"

The Salon: a journal of poetry & fiction: "At the Place Where Hope Is a Vestigial but Torn Muscle"

With gratitude to Jennifer Clement for the gift of reading and selecting this manuscript to be published. Writers Anna MacDonald (you rolling river), Marylen Grigas, Sue Burton, Anna Blackmer, Judy Chalmer, Florence McCloud, Dayna Lorentz, Alison Prine, Karin Gottshall, Kerrin McCadden, Paige Ackerson-Kiely, Eliot Sloan, Mary Elder Jacobsen, Sassy Ross, Jeffrey Thomson, Major Jackson, Ron Villanueva, Michael Milburn, and Susan Neitlich, thank you for sharing with me the power of your poetry and for listening to mine. Thank you Joyce McGovern, Kip Moncrief, The Foote School, Sam and Jennifer Ferri, and Amy Bloom for your support. And a special thank you to Barbara Smith-Mandell and the editors and designers at Truman State University Press.

Lark and Rowan, I love you and revel in witnessing your precious, wild lives. Andy, thank you for believing and for sharing your life with me. There are still more reasons why I love you.

In the Beginning

the sky stuffed the earth so she couldn't bear her children out.
For aches of time, he lay over her while the gods and thieves waited inside.

I am full, after a hearty swim, of lake water—that ancestor or mime of ocean,
come from the chopped loin of sky.

Sea tides come in like horses frothed at bits and bridle.
In the stiller waters of our lake, rougher breedings surface   in patches gelled
as continents   appearing out of darkness   like sickles.

Daedalus

In the Pen

To hoof sheep to a hillside

is to breed them to know the boundaries of your land.

The bloodline in them senses the borders of place

and somehow, for generations, flocks stay put.

I walk round circles in the circle

of a stone room which Daedalus built. Hatching

inventions on my heels, catching my shadow round a few times

and swallowing each loop as a tightening belt.

The smell I've caught of myself, sheeplike.

Daedalus, riddle me out of my body and into the fold.

Make me unctuous in lanolin with hair kinked as wool.

Shepherd me kindly by your crook, and give to me, will you,

some type of nimbus or circumscription,

a limit line for the want of a child.

The Dancing Place

Daedalus built a dance floor for Ariadne, the princess who died
  three ways.   She skipped
over its pattern, and in another pattern, scuffed the inlay of wood and stone.

  She danced in sorrow and in a ring, her shoulders hooked on two others.
By the brace of arms and the earth's spin, her feet took flight, her heels
    weightless and bare.

    Once, goes the myth, by childbirth,   once by fear
and once by a woven rope around her neck.

            Daedalus plucked only two feathers from
every known bird to make his wings.   In these small increments,
    there was no record of his plan.
See his work in Ariadne's floor.   Any dancer in a round is pulled outward
    and like every weighted thing, if grounded, can lift.

Datum

Among his many inventions Daedalus discovered isinglass,
the dried and crushed powder from the swim bladders of fish.
With water it is glue or pudding.   The plumb line too
      came from he who kept spool and plummet in his pocket.

            See how it is a weighted object and string, my want.

Builders place brass markers in the floor below spires to check the high
      then higher

            plummet against a center.

            I fashion fixed points, Daedalus, and bindings of jute scraps,
wax and glue.   But to drop exactingly from the sky or into the deep
      is the work of gods.
There is no measure for that buoyant line between child and god and me.

Alibi

I found, this morning, a splay of feathers

        nothing of more weight, off-white in the sallow field.

I had seen the bird once, cumbersome, roosted low in a tree

        but never the monster who got it.

Daedalus pushed his nephew Perdix off a cliff and called it an accident.

        The small boy had shown a knack for inventing too.

He made a saw of a snake's jaw, a compass from two bound rods.

There is always ever room   for only one genius.

    Do not be mistaken, there are many ways to outfox our living—

invent as you would an axe or a sail, another myth.

        Say the boy became a partridge,

that low-flying bird who nests never far off the ground.

        Say whatever happened, we slept through it.

Artificer

Make around me a wooden cow.   Cover it with rawhide.

Wheel me, by rope and ring, off to the pasture of the white bull.

This is how monsters are made.

It is all hiding.

It is all crafting beast around beast.

In the cow, my thick neck is erect under the float of wood.

There is a smell of the wet stick of pine on flaps of bristled coat

and of its shavings, those Daedalus never swept up.

How he understood me,   I do not know.

But by his pity or pride, I want.   I need openly as an anemone

out here in a field of grass.

A Simple Machine of Efficiency
and Suspense

From outside, by glint of sun, I see the golden pendulum

as a grave eye or heart holding to the law of weight.

       Daedalus brought to the world the double-beveled axe.

Twin-headed, two bits counterarced by a line of symmetry

pitted on a hickory haft.

   Its swing in the dark, the sharp-bladed iron, stealth. Hear it cut air. Hear

the tick of the grandfather clock.

      Each will ask nothing of us.   By its nature

and ours is set going.   Between trees and time, think of all the things

to make with what's been made.

About Silence

The child lay down and turned away from me
as if saying, *My death be loud!* And I missed it.

That sound waves never break but dissipate
as floating rings gives me comfort.

If I've told one bay of water, I've told them all
that where the soul turned and died is not itself the grave.

About silence, Daedalus says, let it build
the space of itself.   See how it multiplies.

And measure not it,   but what it bears to witness.
Measure, he says,   not it,   but what it has moved.

We Come and Go in Ships

There is no measure for the body's own orders or reflex of death,

                and Daedalus invented the sails on ships.

          Those shrouds and the lines that draw them up, stitched

to hold the current of air,

            catch and make shape of the wind.

A plain cloak, palliative,

           hauls bodies from here to where—

When a man dies, kick his shoes back under the bed

          open his shirt and coin his eyes.

Watch over him for the small things to shift

      the hollows to sink, the bones to rise.

              Says the Great Inventor, by the sails

and what they have moved, there will be a tug on the line.

        Brace your living weight by hands over hands.

The Remains of Something

washed up, amassed like chum

in a casing. A dim system of tracts, red clots and tar

balls of musk.

What slid out like silt was a whale,

a year along, its shape somehow intact.

Daedalus says

the child inside me will swim laps inside laps of the pool,

will make circumferences in the circumference of the sac.

From a great height once,   I thought my heart may not burst

but would drop as a plummet through darkness,   would dive

as the whale inside a whale.

What Space You Stake O Barrenness

               Once come in and pushed back the raw curve
you spread in circumference and throng.
               What you weigh is equal to what you do not weigh
in the metric of flesh and silhouette.

One sweep of a chip axe against marble slightly wet
               and a slit eye opens.   Then, all the world around it.
Spectrums of color in light fall in and bore a widening pupil.

               In these stone representations, absence equals the seeing eye.
In the body, a bleak and empty dilation
               is equal to the grain and pitch of inside stone.

Firsts Born

Families are trundling out of me like monsters.

The firsts born of Gaia were fifty headed and one hundred handed,

there were uglier one-eyed brutes after.

In my dreams, my babies are crook-armed,

long-haired waifs that I stuff back into darkness and forget.

Until they appear in corners,

their heads cocked at a puzzle on the table, shaking a rattle or ten.

When Winter Comes Up

I am stricken with a fear at night.
I want to tie lines between the rooms of the house
to find my way in the dusky light of the low sun.

Trace myself back and forth until
the feel of the thread becomes memory in hand.

It is like a black-sailed sloop and a king on a cliff, this waiting.
This waiting is a lengthening line sounding the dark.

At the Place Where Hope Is a Vestigial but Torn Muscle

The Great Inventor, my Artificer, made around me now

the sweeping and mammoth body of a whale.

                        No turbulence

for the slick-skinned move of the black,

stuffed rubber of me. See me toothed and diving

with a head full of cloudy lube.

                By this, I could catch you,

halfway round the seas. Sound out to you

from years away.   Nose for you as deep as the cold glow

of ocean ground.

          My slippery calf, my yearling. I will find you,

though my heart outweighs the two of us.

In Image

In wooden sculptures, Daedalus The Great Inventor

        unwebbed arms from ribs and fingers from mitt,

split legs and started his statues walking.   He sealed them in quicksilver

        so they'd shiver and point.

      They walked in the way the gods do—

became something else when touching ground.

Likeness, then, is a silver cloak,   a flattery by elements and turns of tools

        and I have thought of my child for some time.

How she would blink back at me, coo as I do and open her mouth at mine.

Daedalus, who picked up wood and made of it his self and kind

          made first figurines of wax,

copies to melt away into practice.

       In that silvering, full bedroom mirror,

who is it there

      falling away and into shape?

We Await You like Passing an Eyeball Between Us

We sit by rocks, bird bodied and old, and pass our vision in circle.

           Do you see what I see? There are three of us,   I trust.

And these rocks are not rocks but troughs our pacing made.

We cannot see our milky bodies or the dimming dusk.

We narrow on a single, central object around which a halo has appeared.

           Mostly,   there are the

pictures of what the other sees clouded with our own.

We have to stay close, near together,

    to touch always or reach to touch

        a passage to make way by or by which to see.

The Great Inventor Made the Sail

but not without its harnesses,

those lines and their purchases

which capture tidings in the arc of cloth.

The length of a baby's umbilical cord

depends on her first movements.

The more she pulls, the longer grows the link.

My child, coming on, was seen first westering

as a foggy bulb on a vanishing point

as a knot of buoyant rigging, and white.

The rough of her I felt as a tug on the line.

In My Dreams

In my dreams I've strung up lines and lines of clothespins

through a birch and sugar bush.

A damp lashing grows through the woods every night,

empty of clothes and swaddling sheets.

The pegs pivot in all directions, weathered and innumerable.

I can't stop myself trailing them in hollows and up hills.

          These dreams are true, of you, a small nub waiting

to be picked out from the mass of shadowy mouths.

And true of me drawing a line round every sturdy thing I see.

True the pins' logic, their transfer of force.   Press one end release

the other.

Father of Invention

Daedalus made a peahen's fan for me
out of cattails and milkweed.

He wove the stalks in cardboard
and punched a hole in his belt

for my waist.
      It isn't pride, but instinct

all of this pretending.
We'd wake early to run the streets.

He'd say, When the day broke
it broke behind us!   Omnivorous,

those of us, a bevy of believers.
He thought under his thousand eyes

we'd roost in the braces of the attic.
He thought I'd never leave, but still fastened

the feathers in the same way a lone peacock's call
is plaintive in the clear of a wood.

Daughter

Daughter, Daedalus will make for you

Daedalus will make for you your inner ear

in the shape of a bony labyrinth.

There is no shadow or direction of space, but there is a vestibule

where waves of sound will lull in your head,

curve around and cock your body alert.

By this, the world will not appear to spin around you;

you will not feel like you are falling from a great height.

With this, you will only fall from me

and when you do, you will hear the rush of your name

and when you do, you will set yourself like a compass

and look up for the first time.

Daughter, I think of you as a tender

I think of you as a tender in a lock.

Between sluice gates at the gulf where salt

and fresh waters merge. You wait for levels to meet

and they pour as easy as tide, as gravity.

You bob, keel at the sill of open water

prone and submerged.

There is a whistle far off; the lockkeeper

says, *Gun it. Make a run.*

And the chamber opens by windlass and pinion

by rings cinching open by will and gush.

You weigh yourself out, turn by banking

and somewhere run ashore.

Daughter, Your home will be

Your home will be in the nook of the bay

where a beluga fossil surfaced

from the muck.   That we were once

connected to the sea does not surprise me

having looked at you looking at you

in the mirror.   I am Atlantic

around the eyes, rough and salt worn

and you are spring fed, drooling

clear-faced.   The mother whale

nudges her newborn calf to the surface for air.

Daughter, At the edge of the yard

At the edge of the yard, the milkweed pods,

in their silent and gauzy way, will open.

Their fan of seeds so like feathers, you will bring them

to your lips to know them.

I will tell you they were gathered during wartime

as stuffing for life jackets,

that in bulk, the seeds are more buoyant than cork.

I am not sure you are not another woman's daughter

by the floss of your white hair coming in

except that I have a tenderness for the milkweed's cupped shell

and for its dried and fibrous roots which can be woven

into a sturdy and primitive rope.

Daughter, You will sleep on a sheepskin

You will sleep on a sheepskin in the corner of our room.

That the yearling ram gave his life for you should be of no concern,

though I will barter many times again in your presence.

Lambs must present themselves nose atop hooves

to leap from the womb without catching. The ewe in labor circles

her pen into a nest.   We come to know another through sound

or patterns of behavior.   You will lie down in the evenings,

the passage to sleep hard fought, but for the feel of fleece

like the rustle of hay and the fat of the wool greasing your cheek.

Daughter, A sliver of copper

A sliver of copper can move if a ray of light beams upon it.
This is a magic I will keep in mind, eyeing your shadow.

There are forces I see and feel and for the first time again—
the involuntary movement, the filament I call

My One.   Your cry from upstairs will lift me.
The shingles on the roof have gotten hot all day.

Daughter, I will not remember when

I will not remember when you learned to turn your head at your name

but will read about a whale whose captor's voice comes, mimicked,

out of the whale's throat.

               From the other room, you will call, surfacing

from sleep.   I will answer in a voice you know by the way you will call.

Daughter, Of the family line

Of the family line, I can offer you this:

a stock of bargemen, half smiles, a high threshold for pain.

Do not doubt that you will be stubborn. You will bump your head

first against my tailbone and I will reach out for you.

That you may be my twin will make some of our line nervous.

We will move, tethered, as all mass moves—

in correlation.

Take hold of my knee.   Pull yourself up.

Daughter, The butchers will slaughter

The butchers will slaughter a flock of old laying hens
and will collect from their guts a bowl of yellow yolks,
unshelled and clustered like grapes.

They will show us breastplate and heart and will carve out for you
the wishbone. It acts like a spring in the sternum of the bird

expanding and snapping taut with the span of wings in flight.
We will dry it on the windowsill and you will wrestle it and pitch

the bone to snap in your favor.   The globes of yolk will surface
each day from the bowels of our chickens, as apt as fulcrums

in their intention.   Daughter, the butchers are nuns.

Daughter, I will show you the rain

I will show you the rain, how it lines itself

up by gravity at the roof lip.

You are learning of the downward force,

asking for a hand at the top of the stairs

not by word but gesture.

        This is how the pull works too

not by its name but by all its presence.

We grow by pulling to stand

        against a spinning ground.

Daughter, The potatoes sprout eyes

The potatoes sprout eyes   and when they do,
I cover them over in loose-tilled dirt.

One of them is half cleaved and bolted
and I split it, at the thinnest place, in two.

Each begets a system of cysts,   piths
of white which pullulate out of sight.

Daughter, let them lie.   That halves of things
unseen parallel us in their own troughs

is enough. Meanwhile makes its own surprise.

Daughter, Twin Suns

Who can tell the difference—
at the spring equinox see the cluster gallop toward the twilight
and fight it back with luminary fists.

       Now a telescope shows each star is itself a pair. Both share
a body between them, a twinned star too.

Be careful where you look.   What can multiply is anything that beholds
firmament and hand.

Each time the day comes up, I am surprised by the confidences of siblings.
The cleaving likeness between each of us, itself a stave in the family,
          wicks more light than our sum.

Daughter, The cold will come

The cold will come to deliver you

as a body surrounded by another.

If you must take hold of me here,

I will meet you

          north as we are.

There are no islands in winter.

Daughter, Where we come from

Where we come from it skips a generation

like a flat stone across a lake.

I see the way you look to the corners of the ceiling and laugh.

Daughter, the antecedent is that the stone rises off water.

Limbo

Day One

The night does not fall

but rises.

It is the day who falls,

the day who holds

so much in it

that by noon

it is on its knee.

Day Four

I woke to the boatman on the dock
screwing in the pontoons beneath him.

I couldn't get up for the clarity of the ceiling,
the blue walls and that you were still sleeping.

The chaos of the unmade bed and the drying oatmeal
are units of time and duty.   They do not bode well

for offerings.   One poet broke to his knees at a good poem.
Dear Daughter dear, if ever one came, I would rise.

Day ———

When the heat came up we thought we knew

what to do with our time

but instead were left to be quiet

in a house with only some of the books.

There were stairs up and down—

half flights.

     Counting days is more difficult in the morning,

easier at night when it's been done.

We cannot ask of ourselves too much

when we are just making sense of the sounds of tides

and of all the birds who have begun to circle.

Day, I lost a few

and have come back a little later

each evening, like tide.

I'll brim when I'm pulled upright by something.

That I cannot call out to a neighbor

is new and so I make my patterns loud.

Day Six

It is all making sense in the sand.

The tributaries are greedy for their depression.

It is ospreys above us.

Their eyes, black hooded, unequivocal.

From the woven nest on the pitchforked

line tower, they see the bay and where

the sound hooks out to the deep.

And what else? A mismatched sock,

half-empty beer can and a towel on the rail.

The tableaux of our life. What we have to show.

More likely, the wash of these days over my head.

Day Six

Lift a rock and the wiggling ground reveals a hiding place.

That the estuary itself is a rock which a greater mass pulls up at eventide

is another way of thinking about death or time or rhythm

or more likely, patience.

       Daughter, these days have another clock master.

Here the night is just another way to call the exposed shore

and midmorning is another word for the brink of it—

Or sleep.

       Sleep is another word for

the loosened kelp whose buoyant belly mimes every wave.

Day Seven

I call the osprey sentinel, kindly
by the way she masks her eyes
and circles above the pine line.

Many people have many things to say
about this river. I am told a trained eye
can see the tides begin to rush in or out.

I train my eye to the shore. I see
that at night we cannot see the water
but what it reflects.

                        This portrait of light
and that the osprey dives for bunkers
schooling beneath are binaries of one fact

which you can float a body on.

Crossing

O stones across the river are you faces too?

Are you the droppings of titans

are you the chorus at the bone gates?

O stones could you hold me

and aren't you ashamed of your bald stare?

Stones, you shelter the tide.

I see it so perfectly, when

this evening, the river pulled up her hem.

We think nothing of the estuary

but of the sea there is room always for comment.

What you reveal O borderland

what you reveal O watermark

is the gate, is a way O obscurity

and I know how to reach across you

by need by rite by archetype.

I see the footholds and how you beckon:

O me, yes me, come climb to the top

of me and watch the water advance.

Nesting

That the osprey is marked, masked about the eye

brings to mind mothering.

       She watches in widening circles, inland and to the sea.

That she can talon driftwood into a rounded nest

is proof of rugged symmetry,

          of what I suspect

is surrounding you, Daughter, the coastline and me.

There is an order for all points to be equally

            distant from a center.

This concentricity makes me reach for you, Daughter.

        Osprey, I saw you dive

by the same instinct.

       There is a mouth holding open for food.

There is an order for the flesh of a center to hold.

Gravity

It is not that we are pulled down, but that we are pulled together.

When the stone was rolled away, what was left was nothing

but burial cloth.

That the linen lay there alone, as if dropped from godly flesh,

made some believe

in falling up and the celestial draw, that

                      nothing in the grave means simply, *not here.*

What is not on earth registers floating upwards as a low-pitched toll

pulling with it the slightest wave or hill.

How ground leaps as the dying rise!

It's no wonder we look up when our clothes drop to the floor at night

as if the very weight of them rising off us is law.

Daughter,
The Prologue

Prologue

I took the skin of my twin for a jacket,

pulled it along my legs as stockinettes,

pocketed its bones and fat in my side

for later. I came out doused

in birthing fluid like neat's-foot oil

to stink like my mother who stunk like a ewe

who has birthed a dead lamb and can be fooled

by the fleece of a dead one

with some bleating orphan inside.

Locked in a pen, she may not know

not to preen, not to foster one not her own.

How she would stretch my arms through knit sweaters,

bonnet my head, butter the scar across my middle,

and wake me to aspirin mashed in strawberry jam,

a steel spoon over my lip like a darkened nipple.

While on my kidney, a sister sac of odd

cells and ends sits like a forgotten cairn,

smelling of something different,

smelling of what my mother called *sick*.

Fever Shed

Within two days of the swarm
of me, I opened my cell doors
to the rioting and packed
sickroom of my twin,

where family codes like flushed bodies
hallucinate side by side,
whose rash and mucusy mass
of chattering teeth

is a kidney, a liver, a coccyx—
and we became a fever shed,
a place where sick incubates,
waits to catch somebody's sleeve.

Twin A

We.

A newly broken egg
a firecracker, cyst-burst—

not the geometries of bloodlight,
but the puff of skeleton behind it
worsted
        dislocated.

    *

Lit up by spindles
that rained out from us
like the red hair
I was born with

      before it fell out.

*

We are primitive fronds
with keels out, huddled over
like a soft wish
          but there are no bones
just torpor and tucks
of membrane.

*

We boundless tidings
can turn into any order—
sacrum,   somite,   spit.

We are no hand of god
but a fist of cells.

*

We are a variable, two,
become three cells
within cells.   Unclasped
on the brow, a harelip.
Cleft at the forehead,

          a cowlick.

＊

Then rucks,

      filament stalks

bowing and erect.

We are at any moment

a sextant, figuring a lodestar—

               a channel of migration

for we constellation of spooks.

＊

We teem like lice,

are a ring of raised dots

around the shape of a neck.

    Here is where you will hang onto me.

As not a quickening cramp

but a flash of fever.

＊

We see each other by pits

        not yet eyes. Our mouths

            pleat together, we drool

amniotic from the other

in a sac tight as a blister.

※

We are not all

together alone

in the dark world.

※

We glut ourselves,   tumbled

down here.   Twins

but by one furrow of nerve

like a hollow pivot

joint in the swill.

Pits and protrusions;

folding in

furling

unfurling.

Not one host knows we have arrived.

＊

We fold ourselves

by the gut of the other.

Hear—

a tighten

     spurt

          the tighten

               spurt

tightening

of a heart.

Not one

but three.

＊

Behind the scrim of twinship

greed is a constitution

a stout   heartedness;

before there was a heart

we were layers of skin

growing   nerves.

*

Greed opens like a hooked
stubborn burr.
    My lips round yours
suckle my way
    to my own heelprint
kick in mother's rib.

*

Your head is framed like a set ruby—
        by the vaulted plates of your crown
your face folds in sinuses.
        I cannot catch your eye.

Your fontanels feather open,
        worked slack in our saline world.
We, now a frayed tandem.

*

You grow smaller,
    as if cast out on a tender
aweigh in dark and haar.
    One tired line fastens you
to our one cleat above.

*

I dip into our side,
a fluke around you
to pinch you out.

And from the muck of you
I make from an eye an eye,
teeth from a sac of hair beds.

*

A new silence, stillness
where you madly pulsed.
Weightless nudges back
from no one inside
but me.

*

A secret is born.   You anchored
with all your might and mass
as a camouflaged cell
deep in my kidney cluster
and around my waist.

*

The nub of my middle ear grows

    needle head to a north,

feels of what muted turns

    darkness and blood can make.

This is the weight of a god:

    rinds of clotted cells

        embedded with a whirling brain

    and ossifying sutures.

    *

And you, but a curdle

    from a far away nearby,

raised a pocket full of fingers

    and untouched by its weight,

pointed straight at me.

*

Later in a fever fuss

    a knob of three pounds

in my left side

      became the meridian

shift   inside

who   opened

my mouth   to tell.

Twin B, or Teratoma[1]

As mutiny

live in a kidney-to-be

I did rear inside a twinship

the dint of frenzy.

*

Like the grey-eyed one

born from the head

of her father, full grown

in armor and come tapping,

I, the one misbegotten

in the begetting, am a Chaos,

a yawn when this body world began.

Am Teratoma, the flesh made monster.

---

1. A tumor formed of cells of distinct heterogeneous tissues foreign to the site of the tumor and rising
from an embryological abnormality. From *terato*—Greek for "monster."

＊

A gibbous bulb

a cobble of lawlessness

    I am to be, to be

not a spear

but a fisthead,

a sistermass seen

as a kick from within.

    ＊

We doubled in twinship

and in doubling

you swallowed me

by folds of skin

tucked me in,

and kept growing.

I turned on myself

a mouth of tail

tail of mouth.

＊

In our rash chambers

I came unto you

as a scapegrace

a smalling pock of din

simple as chance.

A ball of bedlam

in the side of an innocent babe.

＊

There was no other place but inside you

for myself to be sealed in self.

No other place for the beginning of we.

Packed so close   sistertwin

how could I not   chaosfuss

touch   cinch.

*

And what happens first in the divide of cells

becomes what is and what shall be. I

sistercell was interrupted   was

an amniotic half-life plucked.

And so the earth began without   me fully.

And you   but the one proxy.

*

At our birth, you did cry out

and spread your arms as if falling

to catch your first breath.

Then I did come into the world too

a new place to call new

me embedded in you.

*

We were one and then
cut down the middle

by the great unknown
and its ceremony—

were opened up
        as the cavern
that began the world.

You had me out
        from where
I caught light of you,

brooded on that one line,
        and fattened.

        *

As in the great divide
        of the domed earth: a quarter
water, quarter fire; so was our great split

of skins. What came

     from our cluster

was part you part part me.

     ✳

My name, Teratoma, monster am I.

I, a lot of lonelies, of half hearts.

In the chasm of our body

are mysteries, ones like me

accomplice

unspun

blastocyst.

     ✳

You were the only

sisterself ferried across

the line between

the cloaked shadows and the born.

I swear, on my death

I was meant to be
formed and quick.

*

And so did come
back to you as sick.

Not come loud like war
but hushed as suckling

and silent as if inside
a wooden horse, as if

under the bed, packed
in a fever shed, come

to the place as the Chaos
in body huddled on body.

*

A sistermass

as the vast mouthpiece

of the enclitic fussing

of halves

not all

together alone

in the world

not all

together alone

and come tapping.